I0617382

Do I Have Words For You

A reference book and study guide focused on the correct word choice for business, formal and academic writing.

The right word in the right place at the right time.

By
Michael Carter

First Edition October 2024

Acknowledgments

I would like to acknowledge Helen Parker for her editorial contributions to this book. Her attention to detail and thoughtful suggestions have been appreciated in shaping the final manuscript.

I would also like to acknowledge Rachel Foster for her editorial contributions. Her tireless and timely attention to detail was exceptional and greatly appreciated.

Thank you both.

Table of Contents

Introduction

Purpose

Do I Have Words for You provides an easy-to-use reference book for selecting the correct word or phrase used in written, verbal, and nonverbal communication.

Scope

The scope of *Do I Have Words for You* is to present words that are frequently confused with other words in a manner that makes their correct usage unclear. All languages change over time, and word usage also changes. For example, the word *Internet* is currently considered a proper noun and is capitalized when referring to the worldwide interconnected networks.

The book is designed with a Table of Contents in the front and an Index in the back so the reader can easily find the words or words they are researching.

About the author

Michael Carter was born in Eugene, Oregon, in 1940. His early years were spent in Oregon, California, and Utah. After graduating from Franklin High School in Los Angeles in 1958, he attended Pasadena City College for one year, where he was elected class president. In 1960, he joined the U.S. Army and was stationed at Ft. Liberty (Bragg) in NC, where he completed jump school and became a paratrooper in the 82nd Airborne and was honorably discharged in 1963 as a squad leader (E-5). He then trained as a computer programmer and went to work for United Airlines in Denver, CO. Being a single parent and looking for answers, Carter sold everything, packed up the kids, bought a sailboat, and took a year off sailing in the Bahamas and Caribbean. Carter then settled in Pennekamp State Park, Florida. Later, he commuted to Miami to work at Eastern Airlines on the reservation system and obtained his U.S. Coast Guard Captain's License. After Eastern went out of business, Carter worked as a captain on a variety of boats, including tug and barges, a research vessel, a paddle wheeler, a ferry boat, an air boat, and evening cruise boats. Carter and his wife also delivered boats for people and businesses. Carter then wrote user manuals for the marine industry and received his Master's in Technical Communication from the University of Central Florida. He later received his MBA in Management from Webber University in Florida. In the summer of 2002, Carter and his wife hiked approximately 750 miles of the Appalachian Trail. Carter settled in Lake Wales, Florida, and, from 2008-2012, was elected city commissioner and then mayor. Carter taught English and Business Communications at Polk State College for fourteen years. Carter lost his wife to ovarian cancer in 2021 and is currently retired and enjoys his time traveling and writing.

Tone and Style

Tone

The tone is your current mood and is usually temporary. It defines how a writer or speaker expresses their attitude through written, verbal and nonverbal communication. Tone assists in creating the mood or atmosphere and can change very quickly based on the feedback between the writer or speaker and the audience. Tone is expressed by word choice, transitions, voice inflection and level of formality. Tone can be defined as what the writer or speaker *feels* about the subject and should always be appropriate for the audience and purpose.

Style

Style is your communication personality and generally is more permanent than tone. Style is based on choices about diction, syntax, sentence structure, physical voice, detail, dialogue, literary devices and rhythm. Although closely linked to tone, style can be thought of as the *package* or context of the communication.

Style includes tone and should also be appropriate for the audience.

Audience and Purpose

Always remember the two most important components of communication: audience and purpose. The thesis is the presentation, in writing, of the main idea and is what connects the audience with purpose.

Who will be the primary audience of your communication (written, verbal or nonverbal) and what is your purpose?

Commonly Confused Words

A and an

Use *a* (indef. art.) before words or abbreviations beginning with a consonant or consonant sound, including y, *h,* or *w.*

The office manager resolved *a* scheduling problem.

- It was *a* historic event for the community. (*historic* begins with the consonant *h.*)

- The year's activities were summarized in *a* one-page report. (*One* begins with the consonant sound "wuh").

Some words are pronounced differently in American English and British English.

- She added *an* herb to the recipe. ((The *h* is silent in American English).

- She added *a* herb to the recipe. ((The *h* is spoken in British English).

Use *an* (indef. art.) before words or abbreviations beginning with a vowel or a consonant with a vowel sound *a* and when the ***h*** is silent.

- She was *an* ideal candidate for the job.

- She arrived *an* hour early. (*Hour* begins with a silent *h.*)

- He was *an* honorable man. (The *h* is silent.)

Use an *h* before spoken acronyms.

- He was *an* FBI agent.
- She has *an* MBA.
- He bought *an* SLR digital camera.

Refer to *References for additional* resources on the use of *a* and *an*.

Abbreviate and abridge

Abbreviate (v.) means to shorten by omitting. *Abridge* (v.) means to shorten by condensing.

- She was good at *abbreviations* in her text messages.
- If your civil rights are *abridged,* they've been lessened in some way.

Ability and capacity

Ability (n.) means a developed, actual power. *Capacity* (n.) means an undeveloped potential power.

- She had only fair writing *ability*, but additional college courses helped develop her *capacity* to a higher level.

Accede and concede

Accede (v.) means to give consent or approval or to agree to a request or demand. *Concede* (v.) means to yield but not necessarily in agreement that something is true.

- He *conceded* the race once it was clear he could not win.
- She *acceded* to her manager's request for more information.

Accept and except

Use *accept* (v.) to indicate consent, agreement, approval and admittance to receive or to regard as true and to take when offered.

- I *accept* the new position and all the responsibilities that come with it.

- I accept your offer.

- I can't *accept* your gift.

- Do you *accept* her story?

Use *except* (v. and prep.) to exclude, leave out or to mean "but" or "other than."

- We agreed on everything *except* the starting date.

- I would like to meet with you this afternoon, *except* I have already made plans.

Accountable and responsible

Accountability (n.) is a person's ownership of the result of an event, experience, or specific task. An example of being accountable is requiring the responsible team to individually report on their contribution to the outcome of a project. Accountability comes after a person's responsibilities are complete.

Responsibility (n.) emphasizes tasks, whereas accountability is about results. Responsibility helps employees and participants understand their roles.

Advantage and benefit

Advantage (n.) means a superior position. *Benefit* (n.) means a favor conferred or earned.

- She had an *advantage* in experience over the other candidates.

- The rules were changed for his *benefit*.

Adverse and averse

Adverse (adv.) means unfavorable. *Averse* (adj.) means reluctant or opposed.

- He predicted *adverse* weather.
- She is *averse* to change.

Advocate and proponent

An *advocate* (n.) is a person who defends or maintains a cause or proposal, one who pleads the cause of another before a tribunal or judicial court. The two words can generally be used interchangeably.

- He was clearly an *advocate* for the new redistricting map.
- She is definitely a consumer *advocate*.

Proponent (n.) is a person who argues in favor of something.

Affect and effect

Use *affect* (v.) to mean "to influence" or "to change" something.

- The storm knocked down power lines, *affecting* several thousand people in the area.

Use *effect* (n.) to describe something that happens due to a cause, such as a result.

- Gauging the storm's *effect* requires assessing economic activity that might be lost.

Agnostic and atheist

An *agnostic* (n.) is a person who holds the view that any ultimate reality (such as God) is unknown and probably unknowable.

An *atheist* (n.) is a person who believes there is no god nor any gods.

Aid and support

Aid (v.) is a synonym for help and means to assist or to provide *support*. As a noun *aid* typically means assistance from a person or thing that provides help. *Aide* is only used as a noun, typically to refer to people who are paid to assist others. *Aid* and *support* can generally be used interchangeably.

A lot and alot

A lot should not be written as one word (*alot*); write the phrase as two words: *a lot*. The phrase *a lot* is very informal and should generally not be used in business and academic writing.

- The new guidelines showed ~~a lot of~~ *many* improvements to the old procedures.

All ready and already

Use *all ready* to mean completely prepared.

- The team was *all ready* for the big game.

Use *already* (adv.) to mean before this time or previously.

- The staff had *already* corrected the shipping order.

All-round and all around

All-round means versatile or general. *All around* means all over a given area.

- The new quarterback was an *all-round* football player.

- The police were looking for evidence for miles *all around*.

Also, as well and too

Also and *too* are both adverbs meaning in addition. *Also* is more commonly used in writing and is less common in speaking. *Also* occupies different positions in a sentence. Use *also* in the front position of the sentence to add a new point or topic.

- It's very humid. *Also,* you can easily get sunburnt.

- I'll call you tomorrow, and we can discuss it. *Also*, we need to discuss who's going to San Francisco.

As well is much more common in speaking than in writing, and is more common than *also*.

- We should reach out to Nancy *as well*. *Too* is generally placed in the end position.

- I thought the meeting went well *too*.

Allusion and illusion

Use *allusion* (n.) to describe an indirect reference.

- The *allusion* was to her opponent's political record. Use *illusion* (n.) to describe an unreal or false impression.

- The scenic director created the *illusion* of a choppy sea.

All together and altogether

Use *all together* to describe things that are acting together or all in one place.

- The new students were *all together* at the orientation.

Altogether (adv.) means entirely or completely.

- The meeting was *altogether* unnecessary.

Alongside and alongside of

Alongside (adv.) means parallel to the side. *Alongside of* means side by side with.

- Mary stood *alongside of* Sue.

- Bill parked the car *alongside* the curb.

Alumni, alumnus and alumna

Alumnus (n.) means a male graduate, and *alumna* (n.) means a female graduate. The masculine plural form of *alumnus* is *alumni*. The feminine plural form of *alumna* is *alumnae*. Use *alumni* when referring to both men and women.

Among and between

Use *between* (prep.) with two items.

- Emily was standing *between* Sam and Adam.

- Ramon divided his property equally *between* **his two children.**

Use *between* to talk about distance and intervals.

- I will be at the college *between* **eight and ten.**

- The distance *between* **wooden studs in new houses in the UK is 350mm.**

Use *between* **before** 'each.'

- There seems to be less and less time *between* each event.

- Insert a space *between* each character.

- There are nine lines *between* each centimeter. Use *among* **with three or more items.**

- Ramon divided his property equally *among* his three children.

- The letter is somewhere *among* **these papers.**

Among and amongst

Among (prep.) and *amongst* (prep.) both have the same meaning, although *amongst* is more common in British, Australian and Canadian English.

Amount and number

Amount (v.) applies to quantities that cannot be counted. *Number* (n.) applies to quantities that can be counted one by one.

- A large *amount* of grain was delivered to the store. Grain cannot be counted individually.

- A large *number* of students attended the conference. The students can be counted.

Another and additional

Do not use *additional* (adj.) as a synonym for *another*. *Another* (adj.) refers to an element that somehow duplicates a previously stated quantity.

- Ten people took the test, and *another* 10 refused.

- An *additional* 20 others refused.

Annual and yearly

Annual (adj.) is generally used for longer periods of time.

- The *annual* meeting is scheduled for next week.

Yearly (adv. and adj.) is used for a specific set of time periods.

- The *yearly* company picnic is scheduled for next weekend.

Anticipate and expect

Anticipate (v.) means to expect and prepare for something. *Expect* (v.) does not include the notion of preparation.

- They *anticipated* a record crowd by adding more seats to the stadium.

- They *expect* a record crowd.

Anxious and eager

Anxious (adj.) means worried. *Eager* (adj.) means keenly desirous.

- She was *anxious* about her first airplane flight.

- She was *eager* to fly again.

Anybody and any body

Use *anybody* (pro.) as one word to refer to an unspecified person.

- When I went into the library, I did not see *anybody*.

Use *any body* as two words to refer to an arbitrary person or body.

- The police were not looking for just *any body*; they were looking for the escaped prisoner.

Anyone and any one

Use *anyone* (pro.) to mean any person at all; similar to *anybody*

- Has *anyone* seen my keys?

Use *any one* to refer to persons or objects.

- *Any one* of the customers could have spilled the glass of water.
- *Any one* of the vases of roses will be a great Valentine's Day gift.

Arbitrate and mediate

Arbitrate (v.) and *mediate* (adj. and v.) should not be interchanged. One who *arbitrates* hears evidence from all concerned and then handsdown a decision. One who *mediates* listens to arguments of all parties and then tries by reason and persuasion to bring the parties to an agreement.

Argue and quarrel

Argue (v.) means to prove something by logical methods. *Quarrel* (v.) means to dispute without reason or logic.

- The opposing lawyers *argued* before the judge.
- The lawyers became emotional and *quarreled.*

Ascent and assent

Ascent (n.) means the act of rising or mounting upward; climbing.

- The mountain climbers experienced a steep *ascent* to the top.

Assent (n.) means to agree, especially after thoughtful consideration.

- The patient *assented* to undergo treatment.
- She gave her *assent* to the proposal.

Attorney and lawyer

An attorney (n.) is a person who has graduated from an accredited law school, passed the state bar exam, and is licensed to practice law in their resident state.

A lawyer (n.) is a person who has graduated from an accredited law school but has *not* passed the state bar exam and is *not* licensed. Not all states have the same requirement.

Author and writer

Author and *writer* can both be correctly used in business communications.

- Sarah *authored* the proposal for the new client.

- Sarah *wrote* the proposal for the new client.

Technically, an *author* (n.) is someone whose written work has been published. Authors originate the ideas and content of their work. An author can also be used to identify someone in business, government and law who has written such documents as contracts, laws and regulations.

A *writer* (n.) is anyone who writes.

All authors can be considered writers, but not all writers can be regarded as authors.

Awaken and woken

Awaken and *woken* are often used interchangeably. *Awakened* is often used in a more active sense and can be used without the auxiliary verb *to be*.

- The loud noise *awakened* me from my sleep.

Awaken is the past participle of the word wake and indicates that waking up has already happened.

- The sunrise seemed to *awaken* a sense of hope within her, signaling the start of a new chapter.

- By the time the storm had passed, the forest was fully *awakened*, teeming with birdsong and fresh scents of rain.

Woken is typically used with the form of the verb *to be* and is more commonly used in passive construction.

- I have been *woken* by the loud noise.

- The baby was *woken* from her nap by the doorbell.

Awaken and *Woken* are often used in literary content to refer to emotions.

- Different images can *awaken* new emotions within us.

Bad and badly

Use *bad* to describe how someone or something looks, feels or sounds and for various forms of "to be."

- He felt *bad* ~~badly~~ about missing class.

- Things looked *bad* ~~badly~~ for his final grade.

Use *badly* to mean poorly and to answer the question "How?"

- The junior varsity played *badly* ~~bad~~ last night.

- Jim limped *badly* ~~bad~~ after the accident.

Because and since

Because and *since* both connect the result of something with its reason.

- She spoke quietly *because* she didn't want her brother to hear.

- We have no dessert in the house *because* you ate all the ice cream last night.

- *Since* you ate all the ice cream last night, we don't have any dessert tonight.

A *because-clause* can be used at the beginning of a sentence to give extra focus on the reason.

- *Because* breathing is something we do automatically, we rarely think about it.

Note: Use a comma after the *because-clause*. Don't use a *because-clause* on its own in technical, academic or formal writing.

Since (adv. and conj.) means from a certain time in the past or after a certain time in the past.

- *Since* the company went public, the stock has risen 100%.

Because, due to the fact and by the fact

The word because is a subordinating conjunction; however, when combined with *of,* it becomes a preposition. *Due to the fact* is a wordy expression that can usually be replaced with *because.*

- I walked home *because* the bus was running late.
- Sharon rescheduled her meeting *because of* a calendar conflict.

Due to is an adjective that describes or modifies a noun. Adding *the fact* is generally not necessary in business and academic writing.

- The company's bankruptcy was *due to* poor financial management.

Big and large

Both *big* and *large* are adjectives that can interchangeably refer to something with more than average size, height, weight or length, such as a *large* house with a *big* yard.

Big is used to describe something of importance.

- The decision to start a new business is a *big* one.

Big is also used in informal situations, referring to 'older' or 'elder.'

- Ashley is like a *big* sister to me.

Big is used to describe a person, organization, city, or center that is powerful or influential.

- Orlando is a *big* tourist attraction.

Big is also used to describe a generous action involving money.

- Millennials are *big* spenders.

Big is used to refer to something of great strength, force, or popularity.

- A *big* storm moved across the lake.
- Adele has become a *big* hit in the United States.

Big is used in certain phrases and cannot be interchanged with *large*.

- It is no *big* deal.
- John was known for his *big* mouth.

Large is used less commonly than *big* and is used with quantity words such as *large* scale, a *large* number, and a *large* extent, and generally refers to greater than average size.

- A *large* house for the neighborhood.

Large is used to describe something more than average in scope and capacity.

- Central Florida is a *large* producer of citrus.

Large is also used to describe something that is liberal and tolerant.

- Eugene had a generous spirit, which was *large* and kind.

Large is used informally to describe boastful or pretentious actions.

- Bill had a *large* ego, which was easily hurt.

Large is used in certain phrases that should not be interchanged with *big*.

- Tyler's ambitions seem *larger* than life.

- Four convicts are still at *large*.

Biography, autobiography and memoir

Biography (n.) is the life history of an individual written by someone else. An *autobiography* is the story of a person's life written by that person. A *memoir* is a collection of memories written from the author's perspective.

Brave and courageous

Bravery (adj.) is more spontaneous than *courage* and involves setting fear aside. *Courage* (adj.) is about having fear, being mindful of the risks, and consciously deciding to do something anyway.

- The young woman saw the small child fall through the thin ice and *courageously* went on the ice to save her.

- She *braved* the elements.

Burned and burnt

Burned and *burnt* are both adjectives, and the paste tense of *burn* (adj.). *Burned* is more common in American English.

- No matter how hard Mary tried, she always ended up with *burned* toast.

But, however and although

Both *but* (conj.) and *however* (conj.) are used to express an exception.

- The Senator voted in favor of the bill, *but* she had serious concerns.

But is a conjunction and is used to join two sentences. A sentence should not begin with *but*.

However is used in the sense of 'nevertheless'. *Although* means 'in spite of the fact …'.

- *Although* she had serious concerns, the Senator voted in favor of the bill.

- The Senator voted in favor of the bill; *however,* she had serious concerns.

Cannot and can not

Although *cannot* (aux. v.) and *can not* are acceptable spellings for both business and academic papers, *cannot* is generally preferred. You would use *can not* when the 'not' forms part of another phrase, such as 'not only.'

- I *cannot* help feeling sorry for them.

- The wind turbines *can not* only create more jobs but also promote a healthier global climate.

Can and could

Can (v.) is an auxiliary (helping) verb often used alongside other verbs to express ability, possibility or permission. In the case of permission, *could* is often more polite than *can,* but they are both grammatically correct in this context.

- She *can* speak Spanish fluently.

Could is the past tense of *can.* In the case of permission, *could* is considered more polite than can.

- *Could* I borrow $10? See can and may below.

- I *could* speak Spanish fluently when I was younger.

Can and may

Use *can* (v.) to express ability or capability.

- *Can* I borrow $10? Do I have the ability?

- *Can* I go with you? Am I capable? Use *may* (aux. v.) to express permission.

- *May* I borrow 10$? Do I have your permission?

- *May* I go with you? Do I have your permission?

Capital and capitol

Capital is a noun meaning a city that is a seat of government, wealth in the form of money and property, capital letters and punishment by death.

- The company's new balance sheet showed a significant increase in *capital* assets.

- The district attorney decided to charge the suspect with a *capital* offense.

- The young business owner discussed his *capital* needs with the investors.

Capitol is also a noun meaning a building housing a legislative body, and often the area surrounding that building is sometimes referred to as Capitol Hill.

- Tallahassee is the *capital* of Florida.

Careful, cautious and wary

A *careful* (adj.) a person tends to focus actions on precision and thoroughness. A *careful* person also tends to be attentive to details, trying to avoid mistakes or errors by being thorough and precise in their actions.

- Jim begged his wife to be more *careful.*

- Being *cautious* (adj.) implies being attentive to potential risks and dangers in a person's actions and taking steps to avoid them.

- Bill is a very *cautious* driver.

Wary (adj.) means feeling or showing caution about possible dangers or problems.

- Dogs that have been mistreated often remain *wary* of strangers.

Case and event

The two phrases *in any* case and *in any* event are both part of the English language and mean *whatever happens* or *whatever may have happened.*

Ceremonial and ceremonious

Use *ceremonial* to explain a proper ceremonial or ritual. *Ceremonious* means carefully observant of ceremony; formally or elaborately polite.

- The priest blessed the baby with a *ceremonial* drop of water.

- He greeted his rival with a *ceremonious* display of friendship.

Chart and map

A nautical *chart* represents hydrographic data providing detailed information on water depths, shorelines, tidal predictions, obstructions to navigation such as rocks and shipwrecks, and navigational aids.

- The captain and crew often referred to the *chart* as they navigated the Bahamas.

The term *map* emphasizes landforms and encompasses various geographic and cartographic products, such as road maps, atlases, and city plans. A map usually represents topographical information. Maps provide no information on road conditions. Both *map* and *chart* can be used by businesses to explain their future plans.

- The father often referred to the *map* as he drove the family across the country.

- The corporate president *charted* the company's future plans to the board of directors.

Childish and childlike

Use *childish* to describe silly or immature actions. Use *childlike* to describe innocent or unspoiled actions or attitudes.

- Pouting appears *childish* in an adult.

- Her *childlike* appreciation of music gave her great pleasure.

Choose and select

Although *choose* (v.) and *select* (adj.) are generally interchangeable, there are several considerations.

Use *choose* to emphasize an individual's volition and free will.

- He *chooses* a path of non-violence.

Choose is sometimes used for choosing multiple items from a set and *select* for selecting a single item from a set.

Select is used when choices are limited to the available options.

- We *selected* the right fork in the road.

Select can imply some notion of competition.

- Stanford *selects* the best students based on essays.

Cite, sight and site

Cite (v.) is most commonly used in the context of facts, sources, business communications, and academic papers. *Site* (n.) is most commonly used in the context of locations and places. *Sight* (n.) is used in the context of seeing and things that are seen.

- Steve did an excellent job on the 'Works *cited*' section of his term paper.
- The patient complained of pain at the injection *site*.
- The doctor said my *sight* had improved.

Close and near

Use *close* (adj.) when discussing something that deals with abstract ideas or qualities, like relationships. Use *close* when talking about physical distance.

- We live *close* to the supermarket.
- Sue was very *close* to her grandfather.
- Her father was a *close* friend of the judge.
- We had a *close* call on the freeway today.
- The child was *close* to tears.

Use *near* (adv.) to describe something a short physical distance away.

Use *near* to describe a short time in the future.

- A bomb was exploding somewhere *near*.
- The time for Jim's retirement was drawing *near*.

College and university

In the U.S., *Colleges* generally only offer associate and undergraduate degrees, such as a bachelor's degree. *Universities* generally also offer master's and PhD degrees.

Compare to and compare with

Use *compare to* to point out differences between objects regarded essentially of the same order, to simply assert two things are alike.

- The economy can be *compared to* a stallion charging at the gate.

- I *compare* getting comments from students in class *to* pulling teeth.

- She *compared* her work for women's rights *to* Susan B. Anthony's campaign for women's suffrage.

Use *compare with* to place two things side by side to examine their similarities and differences and to illustrate the differences a comparison draws.

- The American economy can be *compared with* the European economy to note how military history impacts future economics.

- It would be interesting to *compare* the academic programs at Purdue *with* Ohio State.

- Ann has a 3.5 GPA, *compared with* Jim's 2.9.

Complement and compliment

Complement (n.) means something that completes.

- A nice red wine *complements* a steak dinner.

Compliment (n.) means to praise.

- The professor *complimented* Betty on her proper use of commas.

Compulsory and mandatory

Compulsory (adj.) is something that you must do because it is required by law or a rule.

- In most states, it is *compulsory* that adult front-seat occupants use seatbelts.

*Mandatory (*adj.) is also something that is required by law, rules, regulations, or a standard procedure. In many cases, mandatory requirements are set by authorities or governing bodies.

- It was *mandatory* for Sue to complete the safety training course before starting the new job.

An example of not paying the rent can help explain the difference between *compulsory* and *mandatory.* Pay late and receive an arrears notice and eviction notice (*mandatory);* don't pay at all and receive an eviction notice by the court bailiff (*compulsory).*

Concerned and worried

Concerned (adj.) is the past tense of *concern,* which means anxious or worried to prove a point.

- *Concerned* citizens protested the mayor's proposal.
- She was *concerned* about showing she could do the job.

Worried (adj.) means mentally troubled; feeling or showing concern about what is happening or might happen.

- He was *worried* about the weather.
- There was a *worried* expression on their faces.

Concurrent, consecutive and simultaneous

Concurrent (adj.) is used to describe events that happen at the same time or side by side. *Concurrent* also has several other less common meanings, including "agreeing" (as in *concurrent* testimony), "cooperating" (as in *concurrent* efforts), and "intersecting" (as in *concurrent* lines). In general, *concurrent* implies that things are side by side in some way.

- The lawn-mowing season is *concurrent* with the hot summer months.

Consecutive (adj.) describes events that happen one after another, such as back-to-back. *Simultaneous* is more commonly applied to shorter periods or events to imply that two things are happening together, perhaps even starting and ending simultaneously.

- The varsity team won two *consecutive* championships (meaning back-to-back).

- After working for eight *consecutive* days, Sarah was relieved to finally have a day off.

Simultaneous (adj.) is more commonly applied to shorter periods or events to imply that two things are happening at the exact same time, perhaps even starting and ending at the same time.

- The translator worked *simultaneously* with the speaker during the presentation.

Confirm and verify

Confirm (v.) means to strengthen; to make firm or resolute. It refers to something already believed to be true. *Confirm* can also mean to swear into office and formally install into a position. Their arrest confirms my suspicion.

Verify (v.) means to substantiate or prove the truth or accuracy of something; to prove, find out or state that something is true or correct; especially when there is some doubt about its validity.

- The study had not yet been *verified* by other scientists.

Conscience and conscious

Conscience (n.) refers to the awareness that one's actions are right or wrong.

- Gene has a guilty *conscience. Conscious* (adj.) means alert or awake.
- The investor was fully *conscious* of the risk involved.

Consent and permission

Consent, as a noun, is an agreement between two parties of equal authority. Either party has a right to say no, and the action only occurs if both parties agree. As a verb, *consent* means no change can be made without the consent of all involved parties.

- Both political parties gave their *consent* to the bill.
- The three senators gave their *consent* to the changes in the bill.

Permission (n.) presumes one person has authority over the other.

- The professor gave *permission* to the student to leave class early.

Console, counsel, council and consul

Console, a transitive verb, means to alleviate the grief or sense of loss.

- Eric tried to *console* his sister over the loss of their dog.

Counsel, as a noun, means advice or a legal or professional adviser. As a verb, *counsel* means to advise.

- The attorney offered *counsel* to his clients.

Council, a noun, refers to a group that governs, administers, or advises.

- The building *council* offers *counsel* to dissatisfied tenants.

Consul (n.) is an official appointed by a government to reside in a foreign country, representing and protecting the commercial and legal interests of their home country's citizens and business.

- He was excited to have *been* appointed *consul* to the neighboring country.

Continuous, continually and continuously

Use *continuous* (adj.) to mark uninterrupted extension in space, time or sequence.

- The whole performance is enacted in one *continuous* movement.

- The batteries provide enough power for up to five hours of *continuous* use.

Use *continuously* (adv.) for a certain duration, uninterrupted or unbroken.

- The fans screamed *continuously* for two minutes after the touchdown.

Use *continually* (adv.) to express on and off with interruptions, happening over and over or frequently repeated.

- Writing well requires you to write *continually*.

Contrast and compare

Contrast (v.) is used to show *differences* between two things that are related in some way.

- I observed an interesting *contrast* in teaching styles between the two women.

Compare (v.) is used to show similarities between two things that are related in some way.

- I *compared* the teaching styles of the two men.

Correct and proper

Correct (adj.) means free from error, in accordance with fact or truth.

- Make sure you have been given the *correct* information.

Correct as a verb means an error or fault put right.

- The Council issued a statement *correcting* some points in the press reports.

Proper (adj.) means adapted or appropriate to the circumstances; suitable because of custom and manners.

- It was the *proper* time to plant strawberries.
- There is a *proper* way to dress for a wedding.

Curious and inquisitive

Curious and *inquisitive* are both adjectives that mean eager to learn new things and can be used interchangeably.

- He was *curious* about the outcome of the experiment.
- She was very *inquisitive* as a child.

Currently and presently

Currently (adv.) means occurring or existing at the present time.

- *Currently*, I am learning to play the piano. *Presently* (adv.) means before long.
- I cannot attend to the matter currently, but I will *presently*.

Customer and client

Customer (n.) is someone who pays for goods or services.

- The firm realized they would need to attract more *customers* who would spend more money.

Client (n.) is someone receiving advice or help from someone else such as a doctor or attorney.

- The attorney welcomed her new *client* into the office.

Data and datum

Datum is the singular form of *data*. Both *data* and *datum* define an item or items of factual information.

- The pieces of information were placed in a database so the *data* could be analyzed.

- One piece of *datum* stood out among the *data*.

Defuse and diffuse

Defuse (v.) literally means to take the fuse out of a bomb. *Diffuse* (adj.) means to scatter or spread an item over a large area.

- The bomb squad quickly *defused* the bomb.

- The early settlers *diffused* westward.

Dessert, desert and desert

Dessert (n.) is a usually sweet course or dish served at the end of a meal.

- The father prepared a delicious *dessert* for the family.

Desert (v.) means to withdraw from usually without intent to return.

- The solider was guilty of deserting his post. (Pronounced like *dessert*). *Desert* (n.) is an arid, barren land, usually without water.

- The *desert* had not seen rain in many years.

Different from and different than

Different from and *different than* are both standard, but some style guides do not recommend *different than*. It is more accepted in business and academic writing to use *different from*.

Different and differently

Different (adj.) is used to describe or modify a noun. *Differently* (adv.) is used to describe a verb, an adjective or another adverb.

- Each student approached the assignment *differently*. *Differently* modifies the verb *approach*.

- Each student approached the assignment with a *different* style.

Different modifies the noun *style*.

Different from, different than and different to

Different from is generally preferred to *different than*. The term *different than* is often used with comparative adjectives such as better, worse, taller, and shorter to introduce a second element in a comparison. *Different* is not a comparative adjective, so *different than* sounds less natural to discerning ears. *Differ from* has been used since at least the 1500s (William Shakespeare's *The Comedy of Errors)*. When in doubt, use *different from*; however, *different than* can be used when what follows is a clause.

- My grandmother looks *different than* I remember.

Different from works best when what follows is a noun

- My grandmother looks *different from* that old photograph.

Difference and disparity

Difference (n.) is the quality or state of being different.

- The defendant seemed to understand the difference between right and wrong.

*Disparity (*v.) is the condition of being unequal and a noticeable difference.

- There can be a *disparity* between what men and women earn in the same profession.

Diner and dinner

Use *diner* (n.) to refer to a certain type of restaurant with inexpensive food, a train car where food is served or a person or persons who are eating.

Dinner (n.) refers to the largest meal of the day and inexpensive frozen meals.

Disinformation and misinformation

Misinformation (n.) is simply false or inaccurate information not provided intentionally.

Disinformation (n.) is false or misleading information provided deliberately to deceive, often in pursuit of an objective.

Dived and dove

Dived and *dove* are both verbs and past tense forms of the word dive. *Dove* is more common in the U.S., while *dived* is more common among British English speakers.

- She *dived* into the icy water.

- She *dove* into the icy water.

Done and finished

Use *done* (adj.) to discuss objects and *finished* (adj.) to discuss people. Remember: The cake is *done* and *people* are finished.

- I am *finished* with my homework.

- I am *finished* with the exam.

- Drain the pasta when it's *done* cooking. The above examples reflect your tone and style.

- I am *finished* with him.

Don't and doesn't

Don't, an auxiliary verb, is a contraction of *do not*. *Don't* is used when speaking in the first and second person singular (*I* and *you)* and third person plural (*we* and *they*).

- I *don't* like seafood.

- You *don't* want to do that.

- *We don't* want to leave yet.

- *They don't* have to leave now.

Doesn't is also an auxiliary verb and is a contraction of *does not*. *Doesn't* is used when speaking in the third person only (*he, she* or *it).*

- He *doesn't* like it.

- She *doesn't* want to leave now.

- It *doesn't* look like he'll be leaving anytime soon.

Drank and drunk

Drank (v.) is the past tense of *drink*.

- I *drank* a lot of beer last night.

Drunk is the past participle (following *have* or *had*).

- She had *drunk* three cups of coffee before going to bed.

Dreamed and dreamt

Dreamed (v.) and *dreamt* (irr. v.) are both acceptable past tense forms of *dream. Dreamed* is a regular verb and *dreamt* is an irregular verb. Dreamt is more common in Britain, and *dreamed is* more common in other English-speaking countries, including the U.S.

- When I was young, I *dreamed* of becoming a famous musician.

Each and every

Each (adj. and pro.) is used when there are only two objects in question and when seeing members of a group as individuals.

Sara wore anklets on *each* ankle.

I visit my mother *each* week.

She watered *each* plant.

Every (adj.) is used to refer to each individual or part of a group without exception.

- *Every* animal is sensitive.

- The magazine is published *every* week.

When the quantifier refers to more than two objects, *each* and *every* can sometimes be used interchangeably and for emphasis.

- The bride received *each* item on her registry.

- The bride received *every* item on her registry.

- The bride received *each* and *every* item on her registry. This is not considered acceptable in formal writing.

- I have my coffee here *every* day.

Each other and one another

Each other (ref. pro.) suggests a degree of familiarity that occurs more frequently in fiction, TV shows, and spoken media and *one another* (ref. pro.) is used in more generalized statements, academic, business contexts and newspapers. *Each other* is a better option in daily life and *one another* is used more often in academic and business situations.

- In this class, all students like *each other*.

- In this class, all students like *one another*.

- "People who love each other fully and truly are the happiest in the world. Everything depends on how we love *one another*." *Mother Theresa*

Earlier and sooner

Earlier (adv.) means relating to or occurring near the beginning of a period of time, a development or a series.

- The chairwoman reviewed the *earlier* motion before asking for a vote.

- The package arrived *earlier* than expected.

Sooner (adv.) means at some uncertain future time.

- The chairman told the board the problem needed to be fixed *sooner* rather than later.

Sooner also means a person settling on land in the *early* West before its official opening to settlement.

e.g. and i.e.

The Latin abbreviation *e.g.* (*exempli gratis*) means *for example*; the Latin abbreviation *i.e.* (*id est*) means *in other words*.

Use *e.g.,* to list examples of something that the author has already stated.

- Samantha always eats fruit for breakfast, *e.g.,* bananas, grapefruit or cantaloupe.

- Bill and John always play cards on the weekend (*e.g.,* poker, hearts or gin rummy).

Note: When using, *e.g.* **do not** put *etc.* at the end of the list.

Use *i.e.,* to elaborate a claim already made or rephrase a previous claim to make it more precise.

- It is dangerous to jump rope with your shoes untied – *i.e.,* you could get severely injured.

- Football is one of the most popular sports in the U.S. (*i.e.,* it earns millions of dollars for its sponsors).

The abbreviations should be used, not the Latin words, because they have been used for so long that they are considered part of the English language.

The abbreviations do not have to appear in parentheses and can be placed directly in a sentence. Parathesis is generally used in more formal and academic writing and is generally omitted in less formal types of writing.

Style guides, such as the Chicago Manual of Style and MLA, vary on whether or not to use a comma after the abbreviations. Either style would be considered correct, but be consistent.

Elicit and Illicit

Elicit (v.) means to draw or bring out.

- The professor *elicited* the correct response from the student.

Illicit (adj.) means illegal.

- The suspect was arrested for *illicit* activities.

Embed and Imbed

Embed (v.) means to fix into a surrounding mass, to surround tightly or firmly, to incorporate or contain as an essential part or characteristic.

- The stonemason worked to *embed* the stones in cement.

- Thick cotton was used to *embed* the precious vase in the box.

- A love of color is *embedded* in all her paintings.

Imbed and *embed* are just different spellings of the same word, and both are correct to use.

Emigrate and immigrate

Emigrate (v.) is used when permanently relocating from a home country to a new country.

- George ultimately decided to *emigrate* to Canada from the United States.

Immigrate (v.) means to arrive in a new country after leaving another.

- Her family left Cuba and *immigrated* to the United States during the 1970s.

Eminent and imminent

Use *eminent* (adj.) to describe something of importance and distinguished. Use *imminent* (adj.) to describe something about to happen.

- Near the town hall were several statues of *eminent* men.

- The birth of her child was *imminent*, if not past due.

Empathy and sympathy

Empathy is a noun meaning the ability to understand and share the feelings of another, often feeling things more deeply than if you just felt *sympathy*.

- The jury did not show *empathy* for the criminals on trial.

Sympathy, also a noun, is the act or state of feeling sorrow or compassion for another.

- He had *sympathy* for the loss of her grandmother.

Emulate and imitate

Use *emulate* (v.) to refer to an attempt to equal or outdo. *Imitate* (v.) means "to copy" for good or bad.

- He tried to *emulate* the recent success of his brother.
- She can *imitate* the calls of many different birds.

Ex and former

Deciding whether to use *ex* (n.) or *former* (adj.) to describe how a situation or relationship ended can depend on the circumstances and your tone, style and mood at the time. *Ex* can be used to describe a situation or relationship that ended negatively, such as an *ex-spouse* or *ex-partner* situation. Also, a politician who is now out of office may be unfavorably referred to as an *ex-president*. *Ex-student* does not necessarily suggest a negative situation, especially when used in the context of associations. Combining a college or university's name with an ex-students association or meeting is common and appropriate.

Former is the recommended adjective when the situation or relationship ends favorably, such as *former boss, former girlfriend,* or *former president*.

- Nancy was still friends with her *former* boss.

Everyday and every day

Everyday (adj.) means used or seen daily, ordinary or commonplace, encountered daily or used routinely.

- I bring my lunch *everyday* to work. (*Everyday* modifies the noun "lunch.")

Every day is a two-word adverb phrase that means each day or daily.

- We study *every day.*

- Mr. Smith assigned homework *every day*.

- If you do something *every day* it becomes an *everyday* habit.

Disinterested and uninterested

Disinterested is mostly used to mean "not biased, free from selfish motives."

- If you make too little eye contact, you may seem *disinterested*. *Uninterested* is commonly used to mean not interested.

- I was so *uninterested* in the result that I didn't even bother to look at it.

Farther and further

Use *farther* (adv. & adj.) to express physical distance.

- Tom ran *farther* than Bill.

- Which is *farther*, New York or Los Angeles?

Farthest (adj.) means the most distant.

- Pluto is the *farthest* planet from the sun.

Use *further* (adv.) to express distance figuratively or non-physically, which can also mean "more/additional" and "to advance."

- Nothing could be *further* from the truth.

- Who is *further* along in her research?

- Do you have any *further* ideas?

- This class will *further* your understanding of ethics.

Furthest also means the most distant figuratively.

- That is the *furthest* thing from my mind.

Fast and quick

Fast is both an adjective and an adverb. *Quick* is an adverb that means moving with great speed.

- It was a fast train.

- She loves fast cars.

- We need to have a quick chat before the meeting.

- Use *quick* to refer to something happening in a short time.

- We stopped for a *quick* snack.

- I just need a *quick* answer.

Few, a few, several and couple

Few and *a few* are both used to refer to a small but nonspecific quantity (and, in some situations, may even indicate the same quantity), but the terms are subtly different. *A few* can be used to point out there are some, as opposed to none.

- *Few* are suited for this kind of work.

- Steve said we didn't receive any applications, but we did get *a few*. *Several* is commonly used to refer to quantities between three and five.

- John tried *several* times to return the call to the client.

In its strictest sense, the phrase *a couple* means two. It is commonly followed by *of*.

- I have a *couple* of errands to run.

Between *a couple* and *a few*, *a few* is more flexible; *a few* more commonly refers to higher quantities than *a couple* does.

Fiancé and fiancée

The different spellings are meant to clarify the gender of the partner. *Fiancé* is the husband-to-be, and *fiancée* is the wife-to-be.

Fjord, cove and bay

Fjord (n.) is a Norwegian word that translates to "a long narrow body," and is characterized by steep sides or cliffs and is formed by the glacial process when a glacier washes away the bedrock as it moves down, generally cutting a U-shaped valley in the surrounding bedrock.

A *cove* (n.) is a small, circular *bay* with a narrow entrance.

A *bay* is a recessed coastal body of water that directly connects to a larger main body of water, such as an ocean, a lake, or another bay. A large *bay* is usually called a gulf, sea, sound or bight.

Follow up and follow-up

When used as an adjective with either *a* or *the* immediately in front of the words *follow up*, a hyphen is needed.

- Please give the applicant the *follow-up* forms.
- Have you sent the *follow-up* report to the committee?
- We need to make a *follow-up* call tomorrow. When using *follow up* as a verb, do not use a hyphen.
- Please *follow up* with the applicant.
- Did you *follow up* with the committee?
- Please *follow up* with a phone call tomorrow.

Forward and foreword

Forward is both an adverb and adjective meaning at, near, trending, or belonging to the front.

- Management moved *forward* with the sales plan.

Foreword as a noun meaning a preface or introductory note to a book by the author.

- The editor was relieved to receive the *foreword* from the author.

Gamble and chance

Gamble (n.) is an act having an element of risk.

- The marketing manager knew the new sales program was a *gamble.*

Chance (n.) is something that happens unpredictably without discernible human intention or observable cause.

- After working all night, she needed a *chance* to relax.

Gender and sex

Gender (n.) refers to the role of an individual, male or female in society and refers to the continuum of complex psychosocial self-perceptions, attitudes and expectations people have about members of both sexes. This is known as a *gender* role. The four genders are masculine, feminine, common, and neuter.

- Mary soon realized she was a victim of *gender* discrimination because of her skin color.

Sex (n.) refers to the biological differences between males and females, such as genitalia and genetic differences.

- The couple was glad to learn the baby's *sex* was a girl.

Generally and usually

Generally (adv.) means in a general manner, disregarding specific instances and concerning an overall picture.

- He talked *generally* about his plans.
- She thought she had a *generally* good day.

Usually (adv.) means according to the usual or ordinary course of things, most often, as a rule.

- Because of the heavy traffic, the trip that *usually* takes ten minutes was taking an hour.

Gibe and jibe

Use *gibe* as a verb to express a taunt or sneer and as a noun as a taunting.

- They *gibed* him about his mistakes.
- That doesn't *gibe* with what I thought.

Use *jibe* (v.) to express agreement or to mean a shift in direction.

- The captain *jibed* the ship across the prevailing winds.
- Their stories didn't *jibe*.

Got and have

I *got*/I *have*

You got/you have

We got/we have

Graveyard and cemetery

Graveyard (n.) refers to smaller burial sites attached to a church and a *cemetery* (n.) is just a large burial ground. Despite the word *cemetery* being older, originating in Roman times, it has remained the more popular term between the two.

Hair and fur

The main difference between *hair* and *fur* is where it grows, not what it is made of. Hair length is a trait that's specific to the human species. Humans tend to have long hair on their head and short hair on their arms, while a deer has short hair all over. Also, unlike hair, fur includes a layer of finer, shorter, denser hairs (referred to as *underfur)* through which longer, coarser, more thinly distributed guard hairs extend. Differences between hair and fur are difficult for science to document because most of what science knows about evolution comes from fossils and hair doesn't fossilize.

Hard and difficult

Hard is an adverb that means the physical property of a substance and can also be synonymous with *difficult.*

- The concrete was *hard.*
- The test was *hard.*

Difficult is only used to describe tasks or actions.

- The test was *difficult.*
- It was *difficult* work.

Help, aid and assist

Help (v.) means to give assistance or support to someone or something; to provide something that is useful or necessary in achieving an end.

- How can I *help* you?
- Their mother always *helps* the children with their homework.

Aid (v.) means to provide what is useful or necessary in achieving an end.

- She was always willing to *aid* a friend.

Assist (v.) means support or aid.

- She *assisted* her brother with his lessons.

Hesitant and reluctant

Hesitant (adj.) implies holding back, especially through fear or uncertainty. *Reluctant* (adj.) implies holding back through unwillingness.

- He was *hesitant* about asking her for a date.

- Steve was a *reluctant* witness.

Idea and thought

Idea (n.) refers to a plan or conception formed through mental effort, while a *thought* (n.) is a more general mental process or reasoning. While *thoughts* may occur spontaneously an *idea* usually involves combining multiple thoughts into a plan or solution to an identified problem or question.

- Could you give us an *idea* of the range of complaints you've been receiving?

- Ask me again tomorrow when I've had time to give it some *thought*.

If and should

Use *if* (conj.) to introduce a possible or unreal situation or condition.

- *If* you win the lottery, you should help a charity.

Should (v.) means to be under a necessity or obligation.

- You *should* stop smoking.

If I were and if I was

Use *were* in statements that are contrary to fact. Statements contrary to fact generally start with "if."

- If this *were* a real luncheon job interview, I would not have worn casual business attire.

Were is the proper choice because you discovered too late that the luncheon was a job interview, contrary to fact.

Use *was* when there is a chance the statement is true.

- If it *was* raining yesterday, the swimming pool was closed.

The clause following 'if' is not contrary to fact; the swimming pool closes when it's raining.

Immigrant and emigrant

Immigrant (n.) is used in reference to the country *moved to* and *emigrant* is used in reference to the country *moved from*.

- Millions of *immigrants* came to the United States from Europe in the 19th century.

- My grandparents were Italian *emigrants* who settled in New York in the 1920s.

Implicit and explicit

Implicit (adj.) describes something as being expressed indirectly without anything being stated or written down.

- *Implicit* in the student's letter was her unhappiness about being away from home.

- The parent told the child, "Do your homework, or else."

Explicit, also an adjective, means stated or made clear; expressed directly.

- Her favorite comedy was rated R for *explicit* language and mature content.

- You absolutely can't drink and drive; it's the law.

Incidence and incident

Incidence (n.) means the rate or frequency of a disease, crime or other undesirable thing.

- There has been an increased *incidence* of opioids in younger people.

Incident is both a noun and an adjective, meaning an instance of something happening, an event or an occurrence.

- An amusing *incident* happened at the football game.

- The changes *incident* to global warming are of utmost concern.

Inductive and deductive

Inductive (adj.) reasoning involves forming general conclusions from specific observations and pattern recognition. Observing something happen repeatedly and concluding that it will happen again in the same way is an example of *inductive* reasoning.

- The volcano has erupted about every 500 years for the last 1 million years. It last erupted 499 years ago; therefore, it will erupt again soon.

Deductive (adj.) reasoning involves forming specific conclusions from general observations.

- Everyone in this class is an English major. Jesse is in this class; therefore, Jesse is an English major.

Into and in to

Into (prep.) indicates movement, direction, or action, such as toward and can answer the question "where."

- He threw the papers (where?) *into* the fire.

- She went (where?) *into* the store.

- The children jumped (where?) *into* the swimming pool.

Into can also be used abstractly.

- She was really getting *into* the game.

- He enjoyed turning *into* Frankenstein every Halloween.

In to is an adverbial phrase; *in* followed by the preposition *to* and can be used to replace "in order to."

- The manager sat *in to* (in order to) offer solutions.

- The Good Samaritan turned the wallet she found *in to* the police.

- The thief broke *in to* the car.

- We decided to dine *in to* avoid the crowds.

Investigate and evaluate

Investigate (v.) means to observe or study by close examination and systematic inquiry.

- The police will soon *investigate* the murder.

- The manager promised to *investigate* when we pointed out an error in our bill.

Evaluate (v.) means determining the significance, worth or condition of something by careful appraisal and study.

- We need to *evaluate* our options.

- The professor began to *evaluate* the student's work.

Issue and problem

Issue (n.) is a matter that is in dispute between two or more parties.

- He had an *issue* with his behavior.

Problem (n. adj.) means a question raised for inquiry, consideration or solution; difficulty in understanding or accepting.

- The supervisor had a *problem* accepting the employee's answer.

- Jane was a *problem* employee.

Its and it's

Its (adj.) means 'of' or relating to it or itself, especially as possessor, agent or object of an 'action'.

- The vote on the bill was *its* final enactment into law.

- The dog was seen going to *its* kennel.

- Let the medicine do *its* job.

It's is a contraction of 'it is' or 'it has'.

- *It's* raining. (It is raining.)

- *It's* been raining since last night. (It has been raining since last night.)

I wish I was and I wish I were

The subjunctive mood is used when referring to potential or hypothetical situations, like wishing for something that doesn't exist.

- *I wish I was* still living in the same city as my parents.

- *I wish I were* a millionaire, then I would buy my children each a house.

Jail and prison

Jail (n.) describes a place for those awaiting trial or held for minor crimes.

- He was being held in *jail* awaiting trial.

Prison (n.) describes a place for criminals convicted of serious crimes.

- The man was found guilty by the jury and sentenced to three years in *prison*.

Jealousy and envy

Jealousy (n.) means unpleasant suspicion or apprehension of a rivalry and the fear that someone else will take what you already possess.

- The feeling of *jealousy* took over when she took my husband for a ride.

Envy (n. or v.) is the emotion when you want a possession someone else has.

- I *envy* his situation with a new job.

Just and only

Just (v.) is often used to indicate fairness or impartiality. *Just* suggests something that is precisely correct or perfectly aligned with what is expected or desired, very recently in the immediate past.

- We *just* finished the big project.
- Be careful – I *just* washed the floor, and it's still wet.

Only (adv., adj. conj.) indicates something exclusive for a special or single thing.

- May I have another glass of water? I *only* had one.

Lay, laying and lie

Lay (v.) means to place an object down or refer to an object's location.

- I *lay* down for a nap every afternoon.

- I was told to *lay* the book down.

Lie (v.) means to recline or rest.

- I have a headache, so I'm going to *lie* down.

- The Doctor told me to *lie* down.

- You can *lie* there all day if you want, but the homework is still due tomorrow.

Laying (v.) refers to a direct object and the action to be performed.

- The book was *laying* on the table.

Lead and led

Lead (irr. v.) means to guide, direct or take the initiative. *Lead* is also the name of a certain type of metal, although it's pronounced *led* when it's used for metal. The soft core of a pencil is sometimes referred to as *lead*.

- I hope to *lead* the race after the first lap.

- His legs felt like they were made from *lead*.

Led is the past tense of the verb *lead* and means to guide, direct, be in charge or to bring something about.

- I *led* the race after the first lap.

- She *led* the board meeting through the agenda. Correct.

- She *leads* the board meeting through the agenda. **Incorrect.**

- The accident *led* to an astonishing discovery. Correct.

- The accident *lead* to an astonishing discovery. **Incorrect.**

Less and fewer

Less is an adjective used when referring to something that can't be counted or has no plural, such as money, air, time, music or rain.

- It's a better job, but they pay you *less* money.

- People want to spend *less* time in traffic jams.

- Thankfully, we had *less* rain today.

Less is also used with numbers when they are on their own or with expressions of measurement or time.

- Their relationship lasted *less* than two years.

- Heath Square is *less* than four miles from the Dublin city center.

Use *fewer,* a pronoun, and an adjective when referring to a smaller number of people or things in the plural.

- People these days are buying *fewer* newspapers.

- *Fewer* students are choosing to study science-related subjects.

- *Fewer* than thirty children each year develop the disease.

Lose and loose

Lose (v.) means to misplace from a customary or supposed location or one's possession and suffer a loss or be deprived of.

- *Lose* four games in a row in the NFL, and you're pretty much finished. (Wall Street Journal)

Loose (adj. v.) is used to describe something that is not tightly fitted.

- With the suspect on the *loose*, the police quickly put the neighborhood on lockdown.

Loose (adj.) can be used to describe something that can not be confined.

- The shoelaces on his sneakers were loose, causing him to trip while running.

Loud and noisy

Use *loud* (adj. adv.) to express a sound of great intensity.

- The new employee was *loud* and stubborn.

Use *noisy* (adj.) to express a sound that is turbulent or boisterous.

- The crowd grew *noisy* after the team scored again so quickly.

Matriarch and patriarch

Matriarch (n.) means the female head of a family and *patriarch* (n.) represents the male head of a family.

Milestone and benchmark

Milestone (n.) is a significant event or achievement that marks a specific point in the life of an individual or business.

- The company celebrated a significant *milestone* after posting the five-year sales results.

Benchmarks (n.) function as mini checkpoints to achieve a *milestone*. In business, *benchmarking* is a process that involves measuring the performance of the business against a competitor in the same market. *Benchmarks* can be used to measure and assess the company's progress.

- The staff discussed each *benchmark* in relation to similar competing companies.

More heavy, heavier and less heavy

- *More heavy* (adj.) rain is forecast (**not *forecasted***) for the weekend.

- *Heavier* rain is forecast for the weekend.

- Objects are *heavier* on Jupiter than they are on Mars.

- *Less heavy* rain is forecast for the weekend.

More heavier is a double comparative and is considered **grammatically incorrect**.

Necessary and needed

Necessary (adj.) means something is essential or crucial.

- It's not necessary for you to be here.

Needed (v.) past tense of *need*.

- The company *needed* more space and decided to move.

Need and want

Need (v.) implies that something is essential; anything you really can't do without and maintain your health and security.

- The board chairman reminded the board members of the *need* to approve the new budget.

Want (v.) implies something that is not essential, such as entertainment and travel.

- The board chairman reminded the board members that she *wanted* suggestions on reducing employee travel expenses.

Occasionally and frequently

Use *occasionally* (adv.) to indicate from time to time, now and then, once in a while or irregularly at infrequent intervals.

- Flames could still be seen *occasionally* from the brush fires.

Use *frequently* (adv.) to express that something is happening at frequent intervals.

- As we get older, major arteries of our body *frequently* become thickened with plaque.

Odor, smell, fragrance and scent

Odor is a noun meaning a quality or sensation of anything that stimulates the olfactory organ (the nose) and activates the sense of smell. *Odor* also means a quality or property characteristic or suggestive of something.

- The *odor* of cigar smoke lingered in the room.
- An *odor* of suspicion surrounded his testimony.

Fragrance (n.) means a pleasant or sweet smell.

- The *fragrance* of fresh-ground coffee filled the kitchen.
- Some of the guests thought the *fragrance* of her perfume was too overwhelming.

Smell (v.) means to sense or smell. All *smells*, good or bad, are called odors. *Smell* as a noun means the property of anything that stimulates the nose.

- I *smell* something burning.
- She *smelled* the meat to see if it was fresh.

Scent (n. and v.) means a distinctive odor, especially when agreeable. *Scent* also means an *odor* left in passing by means of which an animal or person can be traced. *Smell* also means to have a suspicion of something.

- The room had a pleasant *scent* of roses.
- The dogs lost the *scent* and the prisoner escaped.
- He *smelled* a rat in the group.

Open and opened

Use *open* as an adjective to mean "not closed."

- I stopped the car when I realized that the back door was *open*.

- The door is *open*.

- The restaurant is *open* all year.

Opened is the past tense of the verb *open*.

- When she *opened* her eyes, she immediately looked at the clock.

Optimum, optimal and ideal

Optimum (n.) means the greatest degree or best result obtained or obtainable under specific conditions.

- This machine has reached its *optimum*.

Optimum and *optimal* are synonyms when they function as adjectives meaning "best."

- We created the machine under *optimum/optimal* conditions.

Ideal (adj.) means perfect or the best possible.

- She's the *ideal* candidate for the new position.

Option and alternative

Option (n.) means an act of choosing; the power or right to choose.

- It was difficult to choose an *option* between the possibilities.

- He had the *option* to cancel the deal.

Alternative (n.) means offering or expressing a choice and existing or functioning outside the established cultural, social or economic system.

- The board was offered several *alternative* plans.

- She was attracted to the *alternative* lifestyle.

Oral and verbal

Oral (adj.) means having to do with the mouth or speaking.

- He stood in front of the class to deliver his *oral* report.

- The dentist gave the new patient an *oral* exam.

Verbal (adj.) means expressed in words, which can be written or oral. *Verbal* for just *oral* is a common misuse. Examples of *verbal* communication include face-to-face conversations, talking on the telephone, public speaking and lecturing.

Paid and payed

Paid (v.) is the correct past tense for *pay*.

- The bookkeeper always *paid* the company bills on time.

- The staff gets *paid* at the beginning of the month.

Payed is a less common and outdated variant of the past tense of *pay*.

Payed is also a nautical term meaning sealing the deck and hulls of wooden ships and handling ropes and chains.

Peaceful and peaceable

Peaceful (adj.) means untroubled by conflict, agitation or commotion.

- The neighbors worked hard to settle their disputes *peacefully*.

Peaceable (adj.) means disposed to peace, not contentious or quarrelsome.

- The crowd dispersed in a *peaceable* manner.

Peak, peek and pique

Peak means the highest or most important point.

- Early morning is the *peak* traffic on the interstate.

- Oil prices reached their *peak* last year.

- The climbers spot they could reach the *peak* of the mountain in two hours.

Peak can also be used as a verb to mean the highest point.

- The politician *peaked* during his term.

Peek as a verb means to look or glance quickly, especially through a small opening or from a concealed location.

- Paulette *peeked* out the window to see who was at the door.

Pique, as a verb, means a sharp irritation or resentment, especially to someone's pride. Also, to excite with interest or curiosity.

- She was greatly *piqued* when he refused her invitation.

- His curiosity was *piqued* by the crowd.

Persons and people

Persons (n.) is generally a plural noun appearing primarily in formal situations such as legal work. Lease agreements use the term *persons* in legal writing on their documents.

- The building occupancy is limited to 200 *persons.*

People (n.) is generally a collective noun and refers to an indeterminate number of individuals.

- The *people* of Gaza were becoming very concerned with the civilian casualties.

Pick and choose

Pick (v.) often suggests a relatively quick or spontaneous selection. It can imply a more casual decision-making process without extensive thought or consideration of multiple options.

- She asked her friend to *pick* a movie to watch.

Choose (v.) is more general and implies a more deliberate or thoughtful decision process.

- The manager had three days to *choose* a project leader.

Power and strength

Power is a noun meaning the ability to produce or generate force quickly, which is a function of time and speed of movement.

- The batter had shown great hitting *power* in previous situations.

Strength, also a noun, means the quality of being strong and the capacity for exertion, endurance and overcoming resistance.

- She was sure she had the *strength* to do what she needed to do.

Preventive and preventative

Preventive (adj.) and *preventative* (adj.) are interchangeable; they're both used as adjectives to describe things intended to prevent something negative such as care, maintenance, and measures.

Preventive has traditionally been more commonly used in medical contexts.

- An ounce of *preventive/preventative* care is worth a pound of cure.

- Failing to perform *preventive/preventative* maintenance could shorten the lifespan of your vehicle.

- If we take *preventive/preventative* measures, we should be able to mitigate the potential for structural damage.

Principal and principle

Principal, as an adjective, means most important. As a noun, the *principal* means a person who has authority.

- The *principal* ingredient in scrambled eggs is eggs.

- The *principal* of the school established the new dress code.

Principle is also used as a noun, meaning a general or fundamental truth or belief. *Principle* also means a scientific rule or law and a guiding rule that explains how something works.

- The company's *principle* of customer satisfaction was based on a long-established culture.

- Water, following the *principle* of gravity, will run downhill.

Proof and evidence

Proof (n.) is a fact that demonstrates something to be real or true. *Proof* establishes certainty and definitively confirms a claim without room for doubt.

- The document was *proof* that her story was true.

- The inventor had to provide *proof* of her invention.

Evidence (n.) is information that might lead one to believe something to be real or true but may not necessarily lead to a conclusive or indisputable conclusion.

- The jury had a great deal of *evidence* to consider before reaching a verdict.

In a criminal investigation, a person's fingerprints on a piece of glass are *evidence*. The conclusion that the person touched the glass is *proof*.

- The police were prepared with *evidence* for the trial.

Prosthetic and prosthesis

Prosthetics (n.) refers to the field of research and expertise in designing and building artificial limbs. It can also be used as an adjective, such as in *prosthetic* limbs.

Prosthesis (n.) is an artificial device replacing a missing body part. The plural of *prosthesis* is prostheses.

Proved and proven

Proved and p*roven* are both past participles of the verb *prove*, which means establishing truth through evidence or argument.

- She is innocent until *proven* guilty.

- I *proved* you wrong.

- I have *proven* you wrong.

Both *proved* and *proven* are considered correct, although The Chicago Manual of Style and The Associated Press Stylebook prefer *proved*.

Purposely and purposefully

Use *purposely* (adv.) to show something is being done intentionally or deliberately. Use *purposefully* (adv.) to describe something being done in a decided manner or fashion.

- She *purposely* kept her thoughts to herself.

- He slammed the door and *purposefully* strode around to the other side of the car.

Quicker and more quickly

Use q*uicker* as an adjective.

- Steve was the *quicker* runner.

- The hand is *quicker* than the eye.

- Frank will find a job where he can make money *quicker*.

More quickly is the comparative adverb of quickly.

- Frank will find a job where he can make money *more quickly*.

- She finished her homework *quickly* before leaving for the party.

References and bibliography

Under the technical definition of a *bibliography*, a *reference* page is a type of *bibliography*. Each is essentially a list of fully written-out citations for all the sources used in a research paper or other work. The *bibliography* is commonly associated with the Chicago format in scholarly work like research papers. The APA format uses the term reference page, and MLA uses the term works cited page.

Regime and regimen

Regime is a noun meaning a form of government or the government in power.

- The opposing party predicted the current *regime* would fail.

Regimen, also a noun, means a systematic plan such as diet, medication or therapy specially designed to improve a patient's health. The r*egimen* also means a regular course of action, especially strenuous training.

- The doctor provided the patient with a strict *regimen* to stay healthy.

Reluctant and reticent

Reluctant (adj.) means to hesitate or feel unwilling.

- We became *reluctant* to drive further when the road became icy.

Reticent (adj.) means reluctant to speak or to be reserved in a manner.

- They call her *reticent* because she rarely speaks.

Renowned and well-known

Renowned (adj.) means widely acclaimed and highly honored.

- She was a *renowned* tennis star.

Well-known (adj.) means fully or widely known.

- She is an anchorwoman so *well-known* that she passes for a local celebrity.

Restrictions and limitations

Restrictions (n.) are limiting conditions or measures, especially legal ones.

- The City Commission placed planning *restrictions* on new commercial development.

Limitations (n.) are limiting rules or circumstances, a restriction.

- She knew her *limitations*.

Rich and wealthy

Rich (v.) typically means having significant possessions and material wealth.

- They lived in the *rich* section of the city.

Wealthy (v.) means more about having sustainable and lasting wealth.

- He came from a *wealthy* family.

Routine and habit

Routines (v.) require a high degree of intention and effort when following a customary or regular course of procedure.

- She was in a *routine* of arriving to work early.

Habit (v.) is an acquired behavior pattern followed until it has become almost involuntary.

- She was in the *habit* of getting up early, doing a 30-minute workout, eating breakfast and getting to school on time.

Sang and sung

Sang (v.) is the normal past tense form of sing.

- She *sang* the anthem.

Sung (past part.) is used only after a helping verb.

- She has *sung* the anthem.

Sea and ocean

Seas (n.) are found on the margins of where the land and an ocean meet and are partially enclosed by land. Seas are generally smaller than oceans. An *ocean* is a large expanse of water between continents.

Seen and saw

Seen is the past participle form of *see* and requires a helper verb such as have.

- We have *seen* this movie before.

- The movie can only be *seen* in theaters.

Saw is the past tense form of see and can be used without a helping verb.

- We *saw* a buffalo yesterday.

Shall and will

Shall and *will* are both auxiliary verbs, also known as helping verbs. They are used together with other verbs to express specific meanings. *Shall* is often used to express intent or determination.

- I *shall* go to the store.

- He *shall* become the next captain of the basketball team.

Will is often used to express determination, inclination or capability.

- We *will* pay the money as promised.

- Caterpillars *will* turn into butterflies.

Showed and shown

Showed is the past tense of show and is sometimes used as the past participle.

- I *showed* you the budget yesterday.

- I have learned from what you have *showed* me.

- She had *shown* me the painting before it was stolen.

Shown is typically the more commonly used of the two, but both are considered standard.

Sight, site and cite

Sight, as a noun, can mean vision or something that is seen.

- The doctor said my *sight* has improved.

- We're hoping to see some beautiful *sights* on our vacation.

- It was a *sight* to behold.

As a verb, *sight* can mean to see, to notice or to observe something you're looking at.

- I'm hoping to *sight* some rare birds on our trip. Use sightseeing, **not** siteseeing.

Site (n.) *means* location

- They visited the *site* of their future home.

- The company has chose a new *site* for office building.

Cite (v.) means providing facts, proof, evidence or examples. In the academic context, *cite* means to quote a passage, especially as an authority. Different formal methods are used in an academic context.

- Authors who are highly regarded by their peers and to be *cited.*

Significant and substantial

Significant (adj.) means having or likely to have influence or effect; a noticeable or measurable large amount, something caused by something other than mere chance.

- There was a statistically *significant* correlation between vitamin deficiency and disease.

- The company faced a *significant* number of layoffs.

- Congress passed a *significant* piece of legislation.

Substantial (adj.) means important or essential; well-to-do or sturdy.

- He ate a *substantial* breakfast every morning.

- She earned a *substantial* salary.

- They lived in a *substantial* house.

Smart and intelligent

Smart (adj.) is an earned status coming from what we learn and study. Being *smart* is quickly adapting to a situation and making the best of it. *Smart* can also be used to describe appearance.

- Julia was *smart* to allow extra study time for the upcoming exam.

- She was always considered a *smart* dresser.

Being *intelligent* (adj.) is something with which a person is born with and is measured by their IQ (Intelligence Quotient). IQ measures a person's ability to learn and does not change.

- Javier had always applied his *intelligence* in his chosen career.

Someone, somebody and some one

Someone is a pronoun and refers to an unspecified member of a group of people.

- *Someone* arrived late for the meeting, which delayed its start.

Somebody is also a pronoun and is generally interchangeable with *someone* in most contexts. *Someone* is considered more formal than *somebody* and has fewer syllables.

- The bank required that *someone* authorized by the court sign the document.

Some one refers to an unspecified member of a group of items or people that are being selected for individual attention.

- Will *some one* please turn down the lights for the meeting?

Speak and talk

Speak (v.) means to vocalize one's thoughts or feelings. *Talk* means to converse and have a conversation.

- The teacher asked the students not to *talk*.

- My mother had a serious *talk* with my brother.

- It is essential to *speak* the truth in court.

- Josefina *speaks* English.

- We *talk* to each other every day.

Stationary and stationery

Use *stationary* to refer to something that is not moving or is incapable of moving.

- The horse remained *stationary* while Mary put on the saddle.

Use *stationery* to refer to writing paper cut to an appropriate size, usually with matching envelopes.

- The office manager wanted new *stationery* for the business.

Stop and quit

Stop is a verb meaning to cease doing an activity.

- I *stopped* eating midnight snacks.

Quit implies that the thing you stopped doing was a commitment.

Quit can also mean to end (stop) something habitual, such as smoking.

- I *quit* my job.

- I realized it would be a mistake to *quit* school.

Subject and topic

Subject (n.) refers to the broad theme or area of knowledge that a discussion, text or academic discipline focuses on and is more narrowly defined than the topic. A *topic* is a more specific aspect or point within a *subject* that is being discussed or written about.

Substantial and significant

*Substantial (*adj.) means something is large in size, number or amount.

- She spent a *substantial* amount of money on new shoes.

Significant (adj.) means you have statistically significant evidence to conclude that your result is not simply due to random chance.

- A *significant* number of customers complained about the service.

Supine and prone

Supine (adj.) same goes for *prone* (adj.)

- A person in a *supine* position is lying flat on their back (face up); a person in a *prone* position is lying flat on their front (face down).

Then and than

Use *than* to refer to an element of time, such as *next* or *at that time*.

- We ate, and *then* we went to the movies.
- Movies were a lot cheaper back *then*.

Use *than* to convey a comparison.

- DVDs are more expensive *than* videocassettes.
- Aardvark is taller *than* Squiggly.

That and which

Use *that* (pro.) when the words following it are necessary to identify the word *that* (pro.) refers to.

- The river *that* flows into the Gulf of Mexico is rising.

Use of *that* identifies the river; without *that,* it would not be clear which river is rising; the sentence would read: "The river is rising."

Use *which* when the words following it are not necessary to identify the word *which* refers to.

- The Suwannee River, *which* flows into the Gulf of Mexico, is rising.

Use of *which* is not necessary because the river is identified in the sentence. The sentence would simply read: "The Suwannee River is rising."

Note: When using *which*, use commas to separate the clause; when using *that*, don't use commas.

Themselves and themselfs

Themselves (pro.) emphasizes a particular group of people or things mentioned.

Avoid using *themself* in academic, business documents and correspondence and formal context; use *themselves* instead.

- It's spring break and the students are sunning *themselves* at the beach.

There, their and they're

There (poss.pro.) names a specific place or location.

- Please get away from *there*.

Their (poss. pro.) means "belonging to them.

- *Their* car is red.

They're is a contraction of *they are*.

- *They're* getting married this Saturday.

To, two and too

To (prep.) is used to show location or motion; it can show movement, direction or limit. *To* can also mean on or upon.

- They went *to* class.
- The dog came *to* me.
- Stop when you get *to* the city limits.
- She applied gloss *to* her lips.

Two is a number that follows one.

Too (adv.) also means more or very.

- He realized he was gaining *too* much weight.

Tortuous and torturous

Use *tortuous* (adj.) to describe something twisted or highly complicated, which means it is neither direct nor straightforward.

Use *torturous* (adj.) to describe something that causes severe physical or mental pain, torture or suffering.

- The mountain road was *tortuous*.
- The suspect was being *tortuous* with his answers to the police.
- The long, winding road was both *tortuous* and *torturous* because of the fatigue and discomfort it caused those who traveled on it.

Traditional and normal

Traditional (adj.) refers to or is derived from tradition; it is communicated from ancestors to descendants only by word.

- We thought her *traditional* values were exceptional.

According to norms or rules, *normal* (adj.) means healthy, not sick at all.

- She soon got back to *normal* after her flu shot.

- It looked like another *normal* day at the beach.

Translator and interpreter

Translators (n.) render the written word from one language to another. They work with different types of documentation, such as novels, medical records, legal documents and others.

Interpreters (n.) work with the spoken word. *Interpreters* work on-site or remotely, interpreting conversations between two or more individuals who speak different languages. They work with courts, government agencies, hospitals and more.

Trooper and trouper

Trooper is a noun meaning a low-ranking soldier or a police officer.

- The *trooper* continued looking for the missing child.

Trouper is also a noun meaning a member of a troupe or someone who persists with difficulty or hardship without complaint.

- The police officer was a real *trouper* when she continued looking for the missing child.

Typical and usual

Typical is an adjective meaning a characteristic or distinctive type.

- She has the mannerisms *typical* of her class.

Usual (n. and adj.) means habitual or customary.

- She demonstrated her *usual* skills on the banjo.
- We experienced the *usual* January weather.

Urgent and critical

Urgent (adj.) means calling for immediate attention.

- The patient required urgent medical attention after the accident.
- He had an urgent desire to resolve the argument before it got worse.
- There was an urgent sense of fear as the storm approached.

Critical (adj.) means to criticize severely and unfavorably; exercising or involving careful judgment or judicious evaluation; being in or approaching a state of crisis.

- They were *critical* of the new policies.
- The citizen gave a *critical* comment on the mayor's proposal.
- There was a *critical* shortage of supplies.

Warranty and guarantee

Warranties (n.) and *guarantees* (n.) are promises manufacturers or sellers make to customers. When a product is "under warranty" or "guaranteed by" its maker or seller, it means the company that produces or sells the product backs the quality in some way and may be willing (or obligated) to repair defects, accept returns and issue refunds and/or make exchanges.

A *warranty* is usually a written, contractual promise that attests to the quality of the product for a certain amount of time. Should the product become defective while still under warranty, the company is bound by the *warranty* to repair or replace the item.

A *guarantee* is also a promise regarding product quality, and it may even be written into a *warranty* contract, although *guarantees* are less likely to be written.

Legally, there is little to no difference between warranties and guarantees.

Welcome and welcomed

As an adjective, *welcome* means wanted, appreciated or pleasing.

- You're *welcome*. Not 'You're welcomed'.

Welcomed is the past tense of *welcome*.

- She was *welcomed* in our home.

Well and good

Use *good* as an adjective to mean something is as it should be or better.

Use *good* to modify a person, place, or thing.

Use *well* to modify an action.

Well is an adverb (modifies a verb), and *good* is an adjective (modifies a noun).

- She played the game *well* (*well* modifies "play" (a verb)).

- She played a *good* game (*good* modifies "game" (a noun))

- You did a *good* job. (*good* describes the *job*, which is a noun, so *good* is used as an adjective.)

- If you're having a *good* day, your day is going *well.*

- That was a *good* breakfast.

Use *well* as an adverb to answer the question of *how.*

- You did the job *well.* (*well* is used as an adverb describing how the job was performed.)

- I feel *well.* (*well* is used as an adjective describing *I.*

- Did you do *well* on your exams?

Active voice is used when the sentence's subject acts as the sentence.

The dog wagged its tail. (The dog is performing the action.)

With the five senses – look, smell, taste, feel, and hear – decide if these words are being used actively to decide whether to follow them with *good* or *well.*

When referring to a person's health or well-being, use *well* as an adjective.

- The son asked the doctor about his mother's illness and was told she was doing *well.* (Not *good.*)

When you tell someone to "*Be good,*" you are talking about their behavior.

When you say, "Be *well,*" you express a wish for their health.

Which and what

When posing a question, *which* is used when there are a small or limited number of answers to choose from or when both the speaker and listener can visualize all the possible answers.

- *Which* foot did she break?

- *Which* one of your brothers is the ball player?

- *Which* movie do you want to see? (When selecting from only a few choices known to both the speaker and listener.)

Use *what* to ask a question when there are an unknown number of possible answers.

- *What* movie do you want to see? (When selecting from many possible choices, such as from all the movies in town.)

- *What* country is she from? (When selecting from many possible choices, such as from all the countries in South America.)

However, if the speaker qualified the question by including a region or continent, both *which* and *what* would be acceptable.

- *Which* country in South America is she from?

- *What* country in South America is she from?

Who and whom

Both *who* and *whom* are pronouns. *Who is* used when referring to the subject of a sentence. When a person is the focus of a sentence and has completed an action or is being discussed, they are the sentence's subject.

- *Who* ate the cake?

Whom is used when a person has (or has had) something done to them, and they are no longer the subject of the sentence but the object of the verb.

- *Whom* are you going to meet at the office?

- *Whom* do you like best?

When determining which to use, substitute *he* or *him* in the sentence and let your ear help determine which pronoun to use. *Who* should be used to refer to the person performing the action of the verb.

- *Who/whom* is responsible for the mess? *He* is responsible for the mess sounds better to your ear, so use *Who*.

- *Whom* should be used to refer to the object of a verb or preposition. *(n.)*

Who's and whose

Who's is a contraction of 'who is.'

- *Who's* (who is) coming to the party.

Whose can be used both as an adjective or a pronoun and is the possessive form of *who* or *which*.

- *Whose* dog chewed up my homework?

- *Whose* book is this?

Will and would

Will is used as a *verb* to express future tense. It refers to inevitable situations or events; a request and facts about capacity or ability.

- I *will* do better next time.

- You *will* understand when you are older.

- Lives *will* be lost in future wars.

- *Will* you pass me that dish, please?

- The stadium lights *will* make it easier to see the game.

- John's wife was left out of his *will*.

Would is the past tense of *will;* it refers to the consequences of a hypothetical situation or events, indicates an inclination or desire, and indicates a polite request.

- He said he *would* be doing the dishes.

- His career *would* be at risk if he did not accept the promotion.

- I *would* love to own a new pickup.

- *Would* you like some pie?

Worse and worst

Worse (adj.) is the comparative form of bad, while *worst* is the superlative form of bad. *Worse* compares two items or actions in terms of how bad they are. *Worst* (n. and adv.) expresses the highest degree of badness. *Worse* means *more* bad, while *worst* means *most bad*.

- For *better or worse*, we need to go forward with the plan.

- His schoolwork got *worse* after his parents split up.

- That was the *worst* meal I've ever eaten.

- Yours is bad, mine is *worse*, but his is the *worst*.

Transitions

What are transitions?

Transitions are words or phrases that connect one idea to the next. Transitions can make your organization clearer and easier to follow.

Why are transitions important?

Transitions are important to maintain continuity of thought and to keep the reader focused on the main topic of the sentence.

How are transitions used?

Transitions are used in sentences and paragraphs to show the relationship between the main idea and supporting ideas.

Types of transitions

Transition words can generally be grouped as either *additive*, *adversative*, *causal* or *sequential*.

- Examples of *additive* transitions: also, furthermore, either, neither.

- Examples of *adversative* transitions: but, however, although.

- Examples of *causal* transitions: because, therefore, in order that.

- Examples of *sequential* transition: to begin with, at first, next, finally, previously.

Word Emphasis

When words or phrases need to be *set off* (stand out from adjacent words for emphasis) in your papers or correspondence, you have three options: *italics,* quotes ("double" or 'single'), or **bolding**.

Italics – your first choice should generally be *italics*. Italics are appropriate in most situations because the italicized word or phrase will stand out enough to be noticed yet not be overly distractive. Italics would be considered best for most business correspondence and academic and professional papers.

Quotes – reserve double quotes for quoted dialogue. If you choose to use single quotation marks to set off emphatic words or phrases, ensure there is no quoted dialogue in the same paragraph. Combining the use of single and double quotes for both setting off words or phrases and quoted dialogue can be confusing and distracting to your audience. Single quotes can be effective when used on a recently mentioned word or phrase. For example, consider the following:

- Some of the audience considered the speaker's comment inappropriate, although 'inappropriate' could certainly be an individual interpretation.

Bolding - bolding is easily overused and is perceived as **shouting** on paper. Be very conservative in its use, if used at all.

Numbers

Following the AP Style Guide, numbers one through nine are spelled out, while 10 and above use numerals. Always capitalize a number when it begins a sentence.

- *Three* times, she was asked to clean her room.
- With the new addition, she now owns *twenty-nine* kittens.
- She arrived early for her *10* o'clock appointment.

Hyphenate all spelled-out fractions.

- *Two-thirds* of the students ordered yearbooks.

Don't hyphenate when fractions are introduced with "a" or "an."

- Only a *third* of the voters supported the mayor.

Hyphenate if the age is used as an adjective before the noun.

- Meet my *seven-year-old* daughter.
- My daughter is *seven* years old.

Prefixes

A prefix is a short word placed in front of a long stem word. Even the word "prefix" has a prefix in it – "pre," which means before. In some cases, the prefix has become so widely accepted that the hyphen has been dropped to form a new compound word, such as *unhappy*, *prehistoric* and *exoskeleton*. If the word is a newer creation, there are double vowelsor it appears before a proper noun, a hyphen is needed.

- The art was *pre*-Christian.
- It's the *pre*-eminent jazz club in the city.

Punctuation

Brackets

Brackets are used to clarify or explain a part of the sentence that is not present, especially in a direct quote.

- I read that novel [The Great Gatsby] in high school.

- I can't believe he [Michael Jordan] is here!

Commas

Commas split a sentence, providing cohesion and unity.

Use of commas: although these rules can vary between style guides. Commas are used when writing a list of three or more items.

- I'm going to the store to buy milk, fruit, vegetables and soda. (Some style guides will have you place a *comma* after "vegetables"; be consistent.

When independent clauses (clauses that can stand alone as sentences) are joined by and, or, or but, a comma is needed.

- My sister baked a cake for my birthday, *and* it was delicious.

The two are joined with a comma if an independent sentence attaches a dependent clause (subject and verb but aren't complete sentences on their own).

- When I have a bad day, I comfort myself with a piece of my birthday cake.

If you can remove a phrase from a sentence without changing its meaning, the phrase is considered non-essential and needs a comma at both ends.

- The weather, which was not hot and humid, was perfect for outdoor activities.

When someone is speaking or being quoted, a comma needs to precede or follow the speech. Depending on the order of the sentence, the comma can be inside or outside the quotation marks.

- "The meeting will come to order," stated the chairman.

- The chairwoman said, "The meeting will come to order." Beginning a sentence with an adverb requires a comma.

- Fortunately, the agenda discussions were short and to the point.

Cities, states, streets and countries need to be separated by commas when writing addresses.

- The corporate headquarters is at 573 Main Street, Orlando, Florida, USA 66732.

A ZIP code is not preceded by a comma.

The day, month and year on a date need to be separated with commas.

- The stockholders meeting will be on Tuesday, March 4, 2020.

Ellipsis

The *ellipsis* is a punctuation mark consisting of three dots, either with or without spaces between them. The plural form is *ellipses*. *Ellipses* signals indicate that something has been omitted from quoted text or that a speaker or writer has paused or trailed off in speech or thought. If the omitted part includes the end of the sentence, a four-dot *ellipsis* may be used.

- "Well, that's true . . . but even so . . . I think we can do better."

- "They think that nothing can go wrong . . . but it does."

Hyphens

A *hyphen* is an essential punctuation mark used to join words and show they have a combined meaning.

When two or more individual words come together to form a new word, they create a compound word such as "basket" and "ball" to become "basketball," and "out" and "side" to become "outside." Language is constantly evolving and some compound words that were once hyphenated have eliminated the hyphen, such as "teenager" and "email." Consult a current dictionary for the correct spelling.

When two adjectives come before a noun and are used together to describe and clarify the noun, that is called a *compound modifier*.

- She loved eating *chocolate-covered* strawberries.

- The city has lots of *small-town* charm.

When using an adverb that ends with a "ly," the hyphen is not needed.

- Call a plumber for the *slowly draining* sink.

- We could not hear the *softly playing* music.

Parenthesis

Parenthesis (n.) are used to enclose incidental, supplemental information or comments used to clarify, illustrate or offer a digression or afterthought.

- In a business letter, the salutation and body of the letter are flush left (against the left margin).

- The manager should apologize for his behavior in yesterday's meeting (he was caught in the middle of a heated discussion between two employees).

Use parenthesis to enclose numbers or letters introducing items in a list or outline.

The punctuation used to end the sentence comes after the parentheses.

- The witch was mean to Dorothy (and her friends).

If the parentheses includes a question mark or exclamation point, put it inside the parentheses.

- I like candy (who doesn't?) but you can't eat it all the time.

Conciseness

The goal of conciseness in business and academic writing is to use the most efficient and compelling words. This does not mean using the fewest words possible but using the strongest and most appropriate words possible. This is important because business and academic readers have limited time to read and process their thoughts, messages or papers. For example, the phrase "due to the fact" is four words that can easily be replaced with the single, stronger word "because."

Every word in your paper has a job to do, and if it does not perform well, it should be eliminated or replaced.

Consider these examples:

The professor demonstrated some of the various ways and methods for me to consider in editing the essay that I had written for class (24 words).

The professor demonstrated various editing methods for my essay (9 words).

Conciseness is closely related to word choice and tone.

Acronyms and initialisms

Acronyms are formed by combining the first letter or letters of several words and are pronounced as words without periods.

- SCUBA - Self Contained Under Water Breathing Apparatus

- FEMA - Federal Emergency Management Agency

- ZIP – Zone Improvement Plan

- NASA – National Aeronautics and Space Administration

Initialisms are formed by combining the initial letter of each word in a multiword term and are pronounced as separate letters not words.

- IBM – International Business Machines

- FBI - Federal Bureau of Investigation

- CIA -Central Intelligence Agency

- FYI – For Your Information

Redundant phrases

Consider eliminating the following ~~strikethrough~~ words that are redundant:

ATM ~~machine~~- ATM is an initialism for <u>A</u>utomated <u>T</u>eller <u>M</u>achine.

~~true~~ fact – a fact is already true.

join ~~together~~ – the act of joining brings components together.

~~free~~ gift – a gift is already free.

~~added~~ bonus – bonus indicates something is already added.

~~end~~ result – results always come at the end.

~~final~~ outcome – outcome indicates the end or finality.

~~repeat~~ again – again suggests something is being repeated.

~~close~~ proximity – to be close to something is to be in proximity.

~~most~~ unique – unique implies something like no other.

rise ~~up~~ – when something is rising, it is already going up.

reason ~~why~~ – the reason includes the explanation of why.

~~new~~ innovation – an innovation is something that did not exist before and is therefore already new.

~~unexpected~~ surprise- all surprises are unexpected.

~~advance~~ notice – when someone is given notice, it is already in advance.

Hyphenation

Kinship terms are always hyphenated, such as *great-aunt* and *great-grandfather*.

When a modifier contains an adverb ending in *–ly*, no hyphen is used.

- The Corvette is a *highly regarded* sports car.

Do not use a hyphen following *after* when used to form a noun, such as *aftereffect* or *afterthought*.

- As an *afterthought* she said, "Thank you."

Follow *after* with a hyphen when it is used to form compound modifiers, such as *after-dinner drink* or *after-theater snack*.

- They both wanted to have an *after-dinner* drink.

Word Choice

Word choice can be influenced by tone and style and is closely related to conciseness.

Rule of word choice

The right word in the right place at the right time.

Comparison and Contrast Words
Write this . . . not this . . .

a complete 180	not this . . .	a complete 360 (Places you back where you begin.)
about	not this . . .	at about
afterward	not this . . .	afterwards
air bag	not this . . .	airbag
all around	not this . . .	all-around
all right	not this . . .	alright
also-ran	not this . . .	alsoran or also ran
amid	not this . . .	amidst
among	not this . . .	amongst
anywhere	not this . . .	anywheres
a lot	not this . . .	alot – try *many*
back-to-back	not this . . .	back to back
backward	not this . . .	backwards
because	not this . . .	being that
cancel	not this . . .	cancel out
canceled	not this . . .	cancelled; *canceled* is the accepted spelling in the United States, and *cancelled* is the accepted spelling in Britain, although both are considered correct.

c.o.d.	not this . . .	cod; c.o.d. is the abbreviation for Collect On Delivery
color	not this . . .	colour; *color* is the accepted spelling in the United States, and *colour* is the accepted spelling in Britain, although both are considered correct.
could have	not this . . .	could of
different from	not this . . .	different than
each one worse	not this . . .	each one worse than the next the last than the last
e-book	not this . . .	E-book or ebook
e-business	not this . . .	ebusiness
e-commerce	not this . . .	ecommerce
email	not this . . .	e-mail or E-mail (Use *Email* at the beginning of a sentence)
ensures	not this . . .	helps ensure
everywhere	not this . . .	everywheres
fax	not this . . .	facsimile or facsimile machine
first-come, first served	not this . . .	first-come, first-serve
for all intents and purposes	not this . . .	for all intensive purposes
half hour	not this . . .	half an hour
hardly ever	not this . . .	almost never
having	not this . . .	after having (eliminate the past participle *after*)

I could care less	not this . . .	I couldn't care less
Internet	not this . . .	internet; Internet is a proper noun and current usage is capital *I* when referring to the world-wide network.
in-class	not this . . .	in class when used as a modifier (We will write an *in-class* essay today.). No hyphen needed when *class* is the object of the sentence (Were you *in class* today?)
nip it in the bud	not this . . .	nip it in the butt
nonprofit	not this. . .	non profit, non-profit or not for profit
number	not this . . .	numeric (or numerical) number; it's already a number
okay	not this . . .	OK, or ok *or* Okay The expression should generally be avoided in business, technical, and academic writing. Example: Ms. Smith gave her ~~okay~~ *approval* to the report.
online	not this . . .	on line or on-line
regardless	not this . . .	irregardless
should have	not this . . .	should of
since	not this . . .	being that
statute of limitations	not this . . .	statue of limitations
themselves	not this . . .	themselfs
TV	not this . . .	T.V.

U.S.	not this . . .	US; US is acceptable in headlines
until	not this . . .	'til or til
Website	not this . . .	web-site or Website
webcam	not this . . .	web cm or Web Cam
webcast	not this . . .	web cast or Web cast
whet your appetite	not this . . .	wet your appetite
whether	not this . . .	as to whether
worldwide	not this . . .	world-wide
would have	not this . . .	would of

Avoid use of . . .

Avoid	Try Instead
in terms of	rewrite to eliminate
	The job was unattractive *in terms of* salary. Rewrite: The salary made the job unattractive.
Knowhow	**Skill**
kind of/sort of	to mean "rather," "somewhat," or "somehow."
	Rewrite: "It was *kind of* a bad year for the company." to "It was a bad year for the company."
	Kind of/sort of should be used to mean only "class" or "type."
	We will use a different *kind of* promotion for the new product.

Gender Neutrality

The English language does not have a gender-neutral singular personal pronoun. *He* and *she* are gender specific, and *they* is plural. This leaves us with few choices. We can alternate using *he* and *she* (or *his* or *her*) in our writing, but this can become monotonous and boring to the reader. We can rewrite the sentence.

- Each student should bring his or her project materials to class.

Change to: All students should bring their project materials to class.

The plural pronoun *they* can correctly be used to identify singular subjects when the gender is unknown.

- Each student should bring *their* project materials to class.

- When will the student be here? *They* will be here before noon.

Ethnicity

An ethnicity or ethnic group is a group of people who identify with each other based on perceived shared attributes that distinguish them from other groups. Those attributes can include a common nation of origin or common sets of ancestry, traditions, language, history, society, religion or social treatment. When in doubt of a person's ethnicity, you may want to politely and respectfully ask them what they prefer.

African-American (with a hyphen) should only be used as an adjective.

- She is a beautiful African-American lady.

- Kamala Harris became the first African-American vice president in 2020.

African Americans, also known as Black Americans or Afro-Americans, are an ethnic group consisting of Americans with a partial or total ancestry from any of the Black racial groups of Africa.

Alaska Natives, also known as Alaskan Indians, Alaskan Natives, Native Alaskans, Indigenous Alaskans, Aboriginal Alaskans or First Alaskans are the Indigenous peoples of Alaska and include Alaskan Creoles, Inupiat, Yupik, Aleut, Eyak, Tlingit, Haida, Tsimshian and a number of Northern Athabaskan cultures.

American Indian or **Indigenous American** is preferred by many Native people, though the consensus is that, whenever possible, Native people prefer to be identified by their specific tribal name. In the United States, the term Native American has been widely used but is increasingly falling out of favor with some groups.

Black is the preferred term when referring to an individual's race. The term should be capitalized and used as an adjective, not as a noun. Black and Blacks used as nouns are both considered offensive. *Black people* is the preferred plural form of Black. Black can be used regardless of nationality.

Black Americans see African Americans.

Caucasians are not always white. Skin color amongst Caucasians varies widely from pale, reddish-white, olive or even dark brown tones. Hair color and texture vary, too, with wavy hair the most common.

Colored is a racial descriptor historically used in the United States during the Jim Crow Era to refer to an African American. In many places, it may be considered a slur.

Hispanic is a commonly used term to refer to people of Hispanic descent.

Latino is an adjective and a noun that describes a person of Latin American origin or descent, especially one who lives in the United States. Latina is used to describe a woman.

Nationality means what country is on your passport and birth certificate. All persons born in the United States are U.S. citizens, regardless of the tax or immigration status of a person's parents.

Native American – see American Indian.

Native Hawaiian means any individual who is a citizen of the United States and a descendant of the aboriginal people, who prior to 1778, occupied and exercised sovereignty in the area that now constitutes the State of Hawaii.

Negro was considered appropriate for use in the early 20th century and now has negative connotations for many audiences. However, in specific contexts and when used with care and consideration, the word can be seen as an important part of historical and cultural education.

Nigger is considered an insulting and contemptuous term for any dark-skinned person or race and should not be used.

Pacific Islander is a native or inhabitant of the Pacific Islands, especially an indigenous person of Polynesia, Melanesia, Micronesia or a person of Pacific Islands descent.

Persons of color are persons whose skin pigmentation is other than white, significantly darker than what is considered characteristic of people typically defined as white. The term is also used to describe a person who is of a race other than white or who is of mixed race. The term is being accepted in academic writing and speech.

Race – The United States Census Bureau officially recognizes six races for statistical purposes: Alaska Native and American Indian, Asian, Black or African American, Native Hawaiian and other Pacific Islanders, White and people of two or more races.

White is a racial classification of people generally used for those of primarily European ancestry.

Parts of Speech

There are eight parts of speech in the English language.

Nouns

Nouns (n.) make up the largest class of words in most languages, including English. A *noun* is a word that refers to a thing, a person, an animal, a place, a quality, an idea or an action. It's usually a single word but not always.

Common Noun

A *common noun* names a general class of things and does not begin with a capital letter, such as an earthquake or army.

Proper Noun

A *proper noun* names a specific person, place, or thing and begins with a capital letter, such as White House.

Count noun

A *count noun* names a thing considered countable, such as a city or state.

Noncount noun

A *noncount noun* names general things or qualities that aren't counted, such as water or fire. Abstract concepts such as happiness, information or time are noncount nouns.

Collective noun

A *collective noun* is singular in form but names a group, such as a herd or family.

Countable noun

Countable nouns are anything that can be counted or measured, such as citizen or country.

Adjective

An *adjective* (adj.) is used to name an attribute added to or grammatically related to modify or describe a noun.

- The family enjoyed staying in the *log* cabin.
- Frank enjoyed his new *luxury* car.

Verbs

A *verb* (v.) describes an action, state or occurrence and forms the main part of the predicate of a sentence, such as hear, run or study.

- The dog *chased* the ball.

Adverbs

There are five basic types of *adverbs* in the English language: manner, time, place, frequency and degree.

Adverbs (adv.) are words or phrases that modify or qualify an adjective, verb or other adverb or a word group, expressing a relation of place, time, circumstance, manner, cause or degree.

- We *recently* bought a new car.
- *So far,* I have found seven grammar mistakes in your paper.
- She hasn't been going to the gym *lately.*
- We went into the haunted house, and there were ghosts *everywhere.*
- She *politely* opened the door for the stranger.
- I was *so* excited to see the new movie.

Conjunctive adverbs are used to join together parts of a sentence to form a larger thought. Conjunctive adverbs are preceded by a ';' and followed by a ','.

- She was driving home from work; *meanwhile,* her husband was busy preparing her a surprise.

Conjunctions

Conjunctions (conj.) are words used to connect clauses or sentences or to coordinate words in the same sentence.

- She bought a new dress *and* new shoes.
- I tried to hit the nail *but* hit my thumb instead.
- I try very hard in school, *yet* I am not getting good grades.

Interjections

Interjections (interj.) are used to express surprise, anger or other types of emotions.

- Welcome.
- Wow!

Prepositions

Prepositions (prep.) generally show how the noun, noun phrase or pronoun is related to another word in the sentence.

- He is a friend *of* mine.
- She wore the dress *with* the stripes.
- The keys are *on* the table.

Pronouns

Pronouns (pron.) are words that replace a noun in a sentence and are used to avoid repeating the same noun again.

- Mike ran so fast; you'd think *his* life depended on it.

Objective pronouns

Objective pronouns such as *me, you, us, him, her, it* and *them* act as the objects of verbs and prepositions.

- Mary saw *her*.
- She waved to *me*.

Possessive pronouns

Possessive pronouns such as *mine, yours, his, hers, ours* and *theirs* are used to refer to something owned by or in the possession of the speaker or by someone or something previously mentioned.

- Thos*e* books are *mine.*

- *Ours* is a family business.

Reflexive pronouns

Reflexive personal pronouns are used to refer to the subject of the clause and include *myself, herself, itself, ourselves, yourselves* and *themselves.*

- Martha fell and hurt *herself.*

- The children had to look after *themselves.*

Subjective pronouns

Subjective pronouns such as *I, you, we, he, she, it, we* and *they* act as the subjects of verbs.

- *She* saw Ma.

- *We* drove the children home.

Pronoun agreement

Pronouns must agree with the nouns to which they refer (antecedent) in gender and number.

- The students submitted their papers on time. (correct because *students* is plural and *their* is plural)

- A student must use pronouns properly in his or her papers. (correct because *student* is singular and *his* and *her* are singular.)

- Students must use pronouns properly in their papers. (correct because *students* and *their* are plural.)

Capitalization of pronouns

The only pronoun that is capitalized mid-sentence is "I". The only exception is the word *God.*

Place names

Place names are the official names of the geographical location, such as a towns, lake or mountainous area and should generally be capitalized.

- The *German* economy is doing well.

- Sue received a set of *fine china* for her birthday.

- John ordered a large plate of *French fries*.

Family names

Always capitalize the titles of relatives when the title is replacing the proper name.

- I'm telling *Mom*.

- We're all going to dinner with *Uncle Bob*.

- Next summer, *Grandma* is coming to visit.

When referring to a relative, but not directly addressing them, use their familial designation.

- My *cousin* loves cotton candy.

- Mary asked her *father* if she could go to the dance.

- You're the kind of *sister* who always protects her siblings.

Titles

Titles that come before names are capitalized.

- *Judge* Smith is going to the ceremony.

- The local *Judge* Jessica Brown is not going.

- *Doctor* Thompson is an excellent doctor.

- *Professor* Jones is an English professor at the local university.

In some business and academic settings, people will always want their titles capitalized.

- Jane Jones is the *Chairperson.*

- James Goodman is the *Executive rector.*

Regions and directions

When referring to a region, the word should always be capitalized.

- The family planned a trip to *Southern California.*

- Because Ann was from the South, she put ranch dressing on everything.

- Alabama and Georgia are *Southern* states.

When describing directions on a compass, use lowercase.

- The directions were to drive *south* for ten miles.

- The *northern* lights are beautiful.

- The weather forecast says warm *southern* winds are coming.

Days of the week, months and seasons

While days of the week and months of the year are capitalized, seasons and periods of time are not.

- *Wednesday* was a heavy rain day.

- June usually has *warm* summer *days.*

- We usually have days of high humidity in *August.*

- During *autumn* we usually have to rake leaves in the yard.

- John arrived late in the *morning* for work.

Periods in history

Archaeological and geological periods are capitalized when referred to by names such as *Jurassic Period, Bronze Age or Stone Age.*

Sentence Structure

There are three types of sentences: simple, compound and complex.

A simple sentence has one independent clause.

- I rode my bike.

A compound sentence has at least two independent clauses.

- I got in my car and I drove into town.

In this sentence, both clauses can stand on their own as complete sentences.

A complex sentence includes an independent clause and one or more dependent clauses.

- I got in my car and then went to town.

I got in my car works as a complete sentence (independent clause), but *and then went into town* does not (dependent clause).

Reference Sources

What are the best reference sources for current word usage for business, formal and academic papers? There are many. Here are a few:

Business Grammar Style & Usage

The Blue Book of Grammar and Punctuation

The Elements of Style Strunk and White

Complete English Grammar Rules

McGraw Hill Education of English Grammer Usage

The Chicago Manual of Style

Oxford English Grammar

McGraw-Hill Desk Reference for Editors, Writers, and Proofreaders

Glossary

Ad hoc

Ad hoc (adv. and adj.) is Latin meaning 'for a particular purpose,' such as a temporary committee organized for one particular purpose.

- The group was called together *ad hoc.*

- The discussions were on an *ad hoc* basis.

Antecedent

An *antecedent* is a word, phrase or clause replaced by a pronoun.

- Jane lost a glove and she (antecedent to *Jane)* couldn't find it (antecedent to *glove*).

Homonym

Homonyms are words that sound the same but have different meanings, such as *right* and *write. Homonyms* can have the same or different spelling, such as *pear* (fruit) and *pair* (couple).

Homographs

Homographs are words that are spelled the same but have different meanings, such as *lie* (untruth) and *lie* (to lie down).

Homophone

Homophones are a type of homonym and are words pronounced the same but differ in meaning and spelling, such as *heir* and *air* or *cell* and *sell*.

Heteronyms

Heteronyms are a type of *homograph* and are words that are spelled the same but have different meanings and are pronounced *differently,* such as *desert* (arid land) and *desert* (to abandon), *tear* (in the eye) and *tear* (to rip).

Ipso facto

Ipso facto is an adverb that means by the fact itself, by the very nature of the deed.

- Because she won the Gold Medal in gymnastics at the Olympics, she was considered *ipso facto* as the best gymnast in the world.

Quid pro quo

Quid pro quo (n.) means a favor or advantage granted or expected in return for something.

His pardon was a *quid pro quo* for his help in releasing the hostages.

Redact (v.) means to censor, blackout or remove parts of a document while releasing the remainder. *Redacting* can include text and images.

- The military will *redact* the document before releasing it, blacking out classified sections.

Bibliography

Aaron, Jane E., 9th Ed. *The Little, Brown Compact Handbook*

Alfred, Gerald J., Brusaw, Charles T., and Walter E. Oliu. 10th Ed. *The Business Writer's Handbook.* New York: St. Martin's Press, Inc. 2012.

Alward, Edgar C., and Alward, Jean A. *Punctuation Plain & Simple.*

Barnes & Noble. 1997

Beason, Larry and Lester, Mark. *The McGraw-Hill Handbook of English Grammar and Usage.* New York: McGraw-Hill. 2005.

Gaertner-Johnston, Lynn. "To Follow Up or Follow-Up" *Business Writing* Syntax Training, 13 Dec. 2016, http://www.businesswritingblog.com/business_writing/2006/03

"The Associated Press Stylebook and Briefing on Media Law" 44th Ed.

New York: Basic Books. 2009.

"The Chicago Manual of Style" 15th Ed. Chicago: The University of Chicago Press. 2003.

Webster's New World Pocket Style Guide New World Dictionaries Cleveland OH 1997

Index

www.ingramcontent.com/pod-product-compliance
Lightning Source LLC
Chambersburg PA
CBHW050443150626
46551CB00028B/1172